It's My State!

WASHINGTON, DC

The Nation's Capital

Terry Allan Hicks and Kerry Jones Waring

Cavendish Square

New York

Published in 2017 by Cavendish Square Publishing, LLC
243 5th Avenue, Suite 136, New York, NY 10016

Library of Congress Cataloging-in-Publication Data

Names: Hicks, Terry Allan, author. | Waring, Kerry Jones, author.
Title: Washington, DC / Terry Allan Hicks and Kerry Jones Waring.
Description: Third edition. | New York : Cavendish Square Publishing, 2017. |
Series: It's my state! | Includes index. | Description based on print
version record and CIP data provided by publisher; resource not viewed.
Identifiers: LCCN 2015045349 (print) | LCCN 2015045150 (ebook) | ISBN
9781627132558 (ebook) | ISBN 9781627132534 (library bound)
Subjects: LCSH: Washington (D.C.)--Juvenile literature.
Classification: LCC F194.3 (print) | LCC F194.3 .H53 2017 (ebook) | DDC
975.3--dc23
LC record available at http://lccn.loc.gov/2015045349

Editorial Director: David McNamara
Editor: Fletcher Doyle
Copy Editor: Nathan Heidelberger
Art Director: Jeffrey Talbot
Designer: Joseph Macri
Senior Production Manager: Jennifer Ryder-Talbot
Photo Research: J8 Media

WASHINGTON, DC

CONTENTS

Official Flower: American Beauty Rose

The American Beauty was chosen as Washington's official flower in 1925. This lovely, sweet-smelling flower has bright petals in shades from deep pink to red, and a long green stem covered with sharp thorns. Some believe it was first grown in America—maybe even in the gardens at the White House.

Official Bird: Wood Thrush

This charming songbird, which has been Washington's official bird since 1960, can be found in wooded areas in many parts of the city. An adult wood thrush is about 8 inches (20 centimeters) long, with white and brown feathers. Wood thrushes eat small insects and berries and build cup-shaped nests in trees.

Official Tree: Scarlet Oak

The scarlet oak takes its name from its leaves, which turn a beautiful bright red color in the fall. Scarlet oaks can grow to a height of 80 feet (24 meters), and they are found all over Washington, DC. The district made the scarlet oak its official tree in 1960.

WASHINGTON, DC
POPULATION: 601,723

★ Key to the City: Opportunity for All

In medieval times, cities often had walls and gates to protect against intruders. Modern cities are no longer guarded in that way, but being presented with the ceremonial keys to the city is a great honor. Washington's ceremonial key was designed by DC native John Dreyfuss and is inscribed with the words "Opportunity for All."

★ Official Motto: *Justitia Omnibus*

These words in Latin mean "Justice for All." They were adopted as the official motto of the district on August 3, 1871, as the first act of the district's first legislative assembly. The words appear on the state seal, which was adopted at the same time.

★ Official Fruit: Cherry

In 2006, students from Bowen Elementary School proposed making cherries the official fruit of Washington, DC. The measure was voted on, approved, and signed by the mayor in July 2006. The students chose the cherry because of George Washington's association with the cherry tree and because Washington, DC, holds a famous cherry blossom festival each spring.

Cherry blossoms brighten the Tidal Basin in the spring in Washington, DC.

The Nation's Capital

One morning in the summer of 1791, George Washington, the first president of the United States, went riding along the Potomac River in Virginia. With him was Pierre Charles L'Enfant, a French-born engineer and architect who had fought at Washington's side during the Revolutionary War. The two men were looking at the place where they planned to build the capital of their new country, the United States of America.

At first, the area did not look very promising. The land close to the Potomac River was mostly swampland, and the areas farther from the river were covered with thick forests. Few people lived nearby. Farms and plantations were scattered here and there. There were only two small towns—Alexandria, on the Virginia side, and Georgetown, across the Potomac in Maryland. Despite all of this, the land was chosen as the grounds for the new capital.

That stretch of land along the Potomac has grown to become one of the world's great cities. It is now home to more than six hundred thousand people. It is the heart of a larger area with a population of nearly six million people. It is the place where decisions that affect the entire world are made. It is the nation's capital—Washington, DC.

Recreational, high school, and collegiate rowers enjoy their sport on the Potomac River.

All three branches of the **federal government**, or the government of the whole country, are centered in Washington, DC. The US president lives and works there in an elegant mansion on Pennsylvania Avenue known as the White House. The Congress meets there, in the US Capitol Building, to vote on the country's laws. The country's highest court, the US Supreme Court, where some of the nation's most important legal cases are heard, is there, too.

Washington, DC Borders	
Southeast:	Maryland
Northeast:	Maryland
Northwest:	Maryland
Southwest:	Virginia

Tens of thousands of people stream into downtown Washington, DC, every day, many of them coming from the city's suburbs to work for the government. They are joined by thousands of visitors from across the country and around the world. Some of these "out-of-towners" come to Washington, DC, to do business with the government. Others come to enjoy all the activities that have made Washington, DC, one of America's greatest tourist attractions.

The Pentagon (*bottom*) and the Washington Monument are separated by the Potomac River.

The District

Washington, DC, is different from other American cities because it does not belong to any state. It is part of a completely separate area, called the District of Columbia—or DC. The land covers 68 square miles (176 square kilometers) and is located on the north shore of the Potomac River. It is shaped like a diamond with one of its corners missing. The state of Virginia lies across the Potomac to the south. On the other three sides of the diamond, the district is bordered by the state of Maryland.

The Potomac runs through the heart of Washington, DC. This great river rises in the Blue Ridge Mountains, in Western Maryland. It flows southeast for 285 miles (459 kilometers) and finally empties into the Chesapeake Bay, a large inlet of the Atlantic Ocean. When the Potomac River reaches Washington, DC, at the Little Falls in the northwestern part of the district, it is still a fast-moving river that challenges white-water kayakers. This section of Washington, DC, is part of a geographical region called the Piedmont. The Piedmont is an upland plain with plenty of fertile farmland. The Piedmont stretches as far north as Pennsylvania and as far south as Alabama.

Adams Morgan

Anacostia

1. Adams Morgan

This culturally diverse and lively neighborhood is located in the Northwest section of DC. It is home to a large number of Hispanic citizens, as well as many immigrants from African, Asian, and Caribbean countries.

2. Anacostia

Located in the Southeast area of DC, Anacostia is a historic neighborhood near the Anacostia River. Its population is mostly African-American. One of its most famous citizens was Frederick Douglass, a leading abolitionist during the Civil War.

3. Brookland

Brookland is part of the Northeast **quadrant** of DC. It is home to many Catholic institutions, including the Catholic University of America, Trinity University, and the Pope John Paul II Cultural Center. Brookland has seen significant revitalization and growth in recent years.

4. Capitol Hill

Capitol Hill is one of the oldest neighborhoods in DC and also one of the most densely populated. It is most well known as the location of the Capitol Building, where members of Congress work and vote on issues, and the Supreme Court.

5. Chevy Chase

This affluent neighborhood is in the Northwest section of DC and is located right next to Chevy Chase, Maryland, a similar town just over the state's border. It is also near Rock Creek Park, a large urban park in DC.

WASHINGTON, DC

6. Downtown

This area is home to many of DC's most famous attractions, including the National Aquarium, the National Portrait Gallery, the Newseum, and Ford's Theatre. The Verizon Center (*right*), a large sports arena, is located there. The NBA's Wizards, the WNBA's Mystics, and the NHL's Capitals play there.

7. Dupont Circle

This neighborhood is built around a large traffic circle with the same name. In the middle of the circle sits a marble fountain, originally placed there in 1920. Most of the houses in the neighborhood are a mix of rowhouses and stately mansions.

8. Foggy Bottom

Foggy Bottom is thought to have received its unique name due to the fog that often results from the nearby Potomac River. The headquarters of the US Department of State is located in this neighborhood. The Kennedy Center for the Performing Arts is also located there.

9. Georgetown

Georgetown is known for its historic landmarks and many academic institutions, including Georgetown University. Famous Georgetown residents from past and present include Thomas Jefferson and John Kerry.

10. U Street

This neighborhood is the place to visit for music, culture, and nightlife in DC. U Street is home to many historic jazz clubs and is an epicenter of African-American culture in the district.

Downtown

Dupont Circle

By the time the Potomac River passes through the center of Washington, DC, it has become a quieter, more peaceful stream. This is because this part of Washington, DC, lies on a mostly flat area called the Atlantic Coastal Plain. This is a low-lying region that stretches along the Atlantic Ocean from New Jersey to Florida. Here, the Potomac River rises and falls with the tides of the Chesapeake Bay.

Other rivers crisscross Washington, DC, too. All of them flow into the Potomac. The Anacostia River runs south through the eastern part of the district. Rock Creek, a much smaller stream, flows gently through wooded parkland in the northwestern section of the district. There is even a stream that lies mostly underground—Tiber Creek, which was covered over when Constitution Avenue was paved in the late 1800s.

The City

Even though it is the capital of a great nation, Washington, DC, has few very tall buildings or skyscrapers. The Height of Buildings Act of 1910 limited the tallest buildings to about 130 feet (40 m). In the center of the city is Capitol Hill. The city's main streets spread out from Capitol Hill, like the spokes of a giant wheel. Located on Capitol Hill is the US Capitol Building, home to the legislative branch (the lawmaking part) of the federal government. Many of the nation's most important events take place here. Every four years, for example, the president is sworn in on the Capitol steps. And it is here, inside the Capitol, that US senators and representatives from all the states meet to cast their votes on important issues. Many other buildings are located on Capitol Hill, including the Supreme Court Building and the Library of Congress.

The Capitol is magnificent in daylight or lit up at night.

Washington's Neighborhoods

Downtown

Many of the most famous sights in Washington, DC, are in the downtown area, near the Capitol. At the foot of Capitol Hill lies the National Mall. Not to be confused with an indoor shopping mall, the National Mall is a 2-mile (3.2 km) –long park lined with trees. Washingtonians love to come to the Mall to eat lunch, relax in the sun, and enjoy everything from a brass-band concert to a kite-flying contest.

Halfway down the Mall is the tall column of the Washington Monument. Every year, more than eight hundred thousand people visit this monument. However, in 2011, the monument was closed for repairs after being damaged by an earthquake. It reopened May 12, 2014.

About 2 miles (3.2 km) away from the Capitol, on the banks of the Potomac at the western end of the Mall, is the Lincoln Memorial. This huge building, inspired by Greek temples, holds a grand statue of President Abraham Lincoln.

The Mall is lined with beautiful stone and marble buildings, including many of the city's great museums. Some of these museums—such as the National Museum of Natural History and the National Museum of the American Indian—are part of the Smithsonian Institution. The Smithsonian is a group of museums, research centers, and educational institutions, most of which are located in Washington, DC.

The National Mall is also the site of one of the most moving monuments in Washington—the Vietnam Veterans Memorial. This simple monument is made up of two black granite walls inscribed with more than fifty thousand names. These names belong to the brave Americans who are known to have died in the Vietnam War.

Northwest

This is the largest part of Washington, DC, both in area and in population. The Northwest includes the elegant row houses of Georgetown. Many government officials have homes there. Washington's Chinatown is also found here, as well as the Adams Morgan area, a place in which many people of different ethnic backgrounds live.

Representatives of dozens of foreign countries work along Embassy Row, which is located on Massachusetts Avenue. This is where the embassies of many countries are located. Embassies are buildings that contain offices for important officials from other countries.

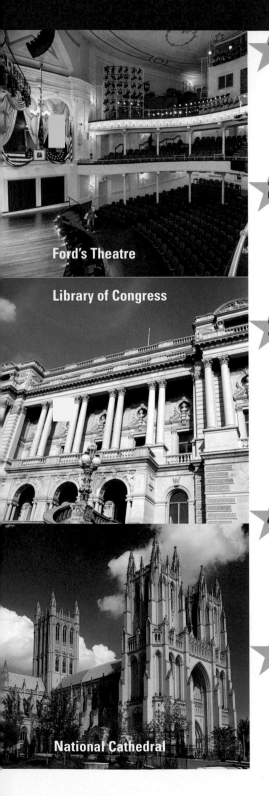

Ford's Theatre

Library of Congress

National Cathedral

1. Chesapeake & Ohio Canal

Known as the C&O Canal, this national historic park on the Potomac River used to be an important path for shipping coal, lumber, and agricultural products. Today, it is a scenic area in which visitors can enjoy nature.

2. Ford's Theatre

Ford's Theatre is best known for being the site of President Abraham Lincoln's assassination by actor John Wilkes Booth. It was shut down in 1893, reopened in 1968, and renovated again several decades later, reopening in 2009.

3. The John F. Kennedy Center for the Performing Arts

The center is named for President Kennedy but it was established as the National Cultural Center by President Dwight D. Eisenhower in 1958. Here you can see many kinds of performances, including live theater and the National Symphony Orchestra.

4. Library of Congress

The Library of Congress houses and keeps track of millions of documents, books, recordings, photographs, and manuscripts. The US Copyright Office and congressional law library are also part of the Library of Congress.

5. National Cathedral

The Washington National Cathedral welcomes people of all faiths to visit. The cathedral, part of the Episcopal Diocese of Washington, hosts many cultural and educational events. When a new president is sworn into office, their inaugural prayer service is often held at the cathedral.

6. National Zoo

The Smithsonian's National Zoo spans 163 acres (66 hectares) in Northwest DC. Asian elephants, giant pandas and exotic birds are just a few of the animals on display. The National Zoo is also dedicated to scientific research that helps us understand and protect our animal friends.

7. Newseum

This interactive museum in downtown DC is dedicated to teaching visitors about news and media from throughout history and today. In addition to the many exhibits and activities available to visitors, the Newseum often hosts important political or cultural events, such as presidential debates.

8. Smithsonian Institution

The Smithsonian Institution is made up nineteen museums, the National Zoo, and nine research centers. Each part of the Smithsonian is dedicated to showcasing different kinds of American culture.

9. Supreme Court

The Supreme Court is the highest level of the judicial branch of the US government. The nine justices who sit on the Court help decide legal cases involving laws of Congress or the Constitution. Visitors can tour the Supreme Court at its Capitol Hill location.

10. The White House

The White House is the home of the president of the United States and his or her family. You can view the White House from the outside by visiting it at 1600 Pennsylvania Avenue.

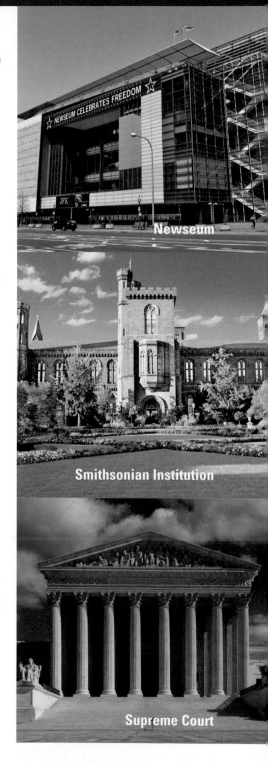

Newseum

Smithsonian Institution

Supreme Court

Georgetown existed before the district, but it is still a busy neighborhood filled with residents and tourists.

The Northwest section borders Arlington National Cemetery, where more than 285,000 veterans from every war in US history are buried. The most famous grave in the cemetery is probably that of President John F. Kennedy, who was assassinated in Dallas, Texas, in 1963.

Southwest and Southeast

The Southeast section of the district is a small, mixed area. There are both large and small homes, as well as national landmarks. One of the landmarks in the Southeast is Cedar Hill, home of the great African-American leader Frederick Douglass. Another area of the Southeast is called Uniontown, which was built to provide housing for the shipbuilders who worked at the nearby Washington Navy Yard. Robert F. Kennedy Memorial Stadium, the former home for many of Washington's professional sports teams, is also found here. It is still the home stadium of DC United of Major League Soccer. The Southwest is the smallest quadrant in the district. It is home to five neighborhoods.

Northeast

The Northeast is home to several neighborhoods where Washingtonians live. It also has many educational institutions, including Gallaudet University—the only university in the world for hearing-impaired people. Another interesting area in the Northeast is Brookland, also called Little Rome, which has more Catholic institutions—such as the Catholic University of America—than any other place in the United States. The Northeast also has public gardens, including the US National Arboretum.

Abolitionist, writer, and speaker Frederick Douglass, an African American, lived in this home in Anacostia called Cedar Hill.

Beyond the Beltway

Washington, DC, is circled by a major highway called the Capital Beltway, which carries heavy interstate traffic around the city. Many of the people who work in Washington, DC, actually live beyond the Beltway, in the surrounding suburbs. Washington, DC, is the center of a heavily populated area that includes large parts of Virginia, Maryland, and even West Virginia. This area, called Greater Washington, is home to almost six million people.

The Natural World

Washington, DC, has preserved its natural beauty better than many big cities. Most of Washington's main streets are lined with graceful old trees. Some of them are familiar species—or types—that have always grown in the area. These include pin oaks, red oaks, lindens, willows, and sycamores. Other trees in the area are exotic imports from other parts of the world. For example, in 1805, Thomas Jefferson, the country's third president, ordered Lombardy poplars from Italy to be planted along Pennsylvania Avenue. Since then, many other foreign trees have been brought to the nation's capital, including acacias, locust trees, ailanthus (also known as "trees of heaven"), and the beautiful Japanese cherry trees. Every spring, Washingtonians and visitors to the district wait for the Japanese cherry trees to blossom. About 3,750 of these beautiful trees, originally a gift from the city of Tokyo, Japan, line the Tidal Basin.

Blossoming Japanese cherry trees bring thousands of visitors to Washington, DC, each spring.

Nearly 150 parks are scattered across Washington, DC. These parks are home to a surprising amount of wild plant and animal life. Skunk cabbages and jack-in-the-pulpits grow beautifully in the marshy lowlands along the Anacostia River. Trailing arbutus, bloodroots, golden groundsels, and Virginia bluebells can be seen all over the city. The parks are also home to many kinds of wild birds, including songbirds such as finches, yellow warblers, and thrushes. Birdwatchers can also see blue jays, chickadees, mockingbirds, and mourning doves.

The usual big-city animals, such as gray squirrels, can be found in the district's parks. These squirrels often beg for food from people walking by. In some places—such as the more remote parts of Rock Creek Park—you might also see foxes, flying squirrels, muskrats, opossums, and raccoons.

However, several of the species once found in Washington, DC, have been placed on the government's endangered species list. The shortnose sturgeon and the dwarf wedgemussel are both considered endangered. When an animal is endangered, its population in the wild is very small. This is partly because of pollution and because the city has spread out into these creatures' natural habitats. The bald eagle, the national bird, was once considered endangered. However, bald eagles have made a great recovery and were taken off the endangered species list in 2007.

In recent years, Washington, DC, has worked hard to protect its natural environment. Many of these environmental efforts focus on the rivers that run through the heart of the city. The Potomac was once so badly polluted by waste from factories and sewers that the

Washington Post newspaper called the river "an open sewer." The fish in the river were badly contaminated by chemicals in the water and sometimes died by the thousands.

Washington's Climate

Washington, DC, has a mostly warm, wet climate. Spring comes early in the district, sometimes as early as late February, when much of the northern part of the United States is still covered with snow.

Summers can sometimes be very unpleasant in Washington, DC. The city is hot and extremely humid from May until September. The average temperature in July is 78 degrees Fahrenheit (25.5 degrees Celsius), but it can seem much hotter because of the humidity. Humidity is the moisture in the air, which tends to make the air feel damp. Heat waves that pass through the city in the summer can push the temperature over 90°F (32.2°C), sometimes for days at a time. Summers are also very rainy.

An average of 50 inches (127 cm) of precipitation, or rain and snow, falls on the district each year. Most of this is rainfall. This is higher than the national average, which is about 40 inches (102 cm).

Autumn is usually a delightful time in Washington, DC. The summer's sticky heat gives way to cooler temperatures. The trees in the city's parks blaze with red, yellow, and gold, and the air usually turns pleasantly cool. One exception came in November 2015, when record high temperatures were recorded. It reached 80°F (27°C) on November 6, the highest temperature ever on that date.

Winter in the district, though, can be difficult and unpredictable, with weather conditions that change quickly. A Washington, DC, winter is often mild, with average temperatures of 37°F (2.8°C). Warm air coming up from the south may make the district so warm that people walk around in light jackets. Sometimes, though, a major storm passes through, bringing extremely cold temperatures and dumping snow and sleet. Winter Storm Jonas, one of the worst ever in the city, dumped up to 2 feet (0.6 m) on the district in February 2016, shutting down the district as cars and trucks were unable to move on the city's streets.

Festival Beginnings

The National Cherry Blossom Festival brings people to DC from around the world, but not many know it was started unofficially by schoolchildren. In 1927, students in DC held a re-enactment of the planting of the city's first cherry tree, an event that was expanded to become the festival.

American Peregrine Falcon

Bald Eagle

Giant Panda

1. American Peregrine Falcon

These birds of prey can fly at speeds around 50 miles per hour (80 kilometers per hour) and can go as fast as 200 miles per hour (322 kilometers per hour) when they are diving. The American peregrine falcon was taken off the endangered species list in 1999.

2. Bald Eagle

The bald eagle is the national bird of the United States. In 2013, National Geographic set up a webcam to let people watch a family of bald eagles living in a tree on the grounds of DC's Metropolitan Police Academy.

3. Deertongue Grass

This grass can grow to be more than 4 feet (1.2 m) tall. It is known for its distinctive wide green leaves. Deertongue can spread quickly and is an important food source for insects, small rodents, and some mammals.

4. Giant Pandas

Pandas are not native to North America, but they have become a symbol of Washington, DC. Unfortunately, there are only about one thousand giant pandas left in the wild. The National Zoo has been home to some of these bamboo-eating mammals since 1972.

5. Hooked Buttercup

This flowering plant grows well in wetlands, making DC's swampy terrain a perfect spot for the hooked buttercup to grow. The hooked buttercup produces yellow flowers and a dry fruit with a hook-like shape.

6. Japanese Cherry Trees

Japanese cherry trees are not native to the United States, but today they are grown in different parts of the country. In the spring, the trees bloom and the district hosts a National Cherry Blossom Festival.

Japanese Cherry Trees

7. Lombardy Poplars

These tall, graceful trees grow in many parts of Europe and Asia. They first appeared in Washington, DC, in 1805, when President Thomas Jefferson had some brought from Italy to plant along Pennsylvania Avenue.

8. Queen Snake

The queen snake is a common reptile in the DC area. It is a kind of water snake that enjoys lying in the sun or in the branches of trees near the water. It eats softshell crayfish—those that have shed their shell but have not yet grown a new one.

9. Southern Flying Squirrel

The southern flying squirrel is a small rodent that is **nocturnal**. Nocturnal animals are most active at night. This squirrel has flaps of skin that allows it to glide from tree to tree. They are very common in the DC area.

10. Sycamores

The sycamore is a type of tree that is native to the Washington, DC, area and much of the eastern United States. Sycamore trees have delicate, light-colored bark and densely packed leaves that look a little like spread-out hands.

Lombardy Poplar

Queen Snake

Archaeologists have found evidence of early Native American residents in Rock Creek Park.

From the Beginning

Native Americans were living in the area that was to become Washington, DC, as long ago as the Paleo-Indian period, around 11,000–8000 BCE. Little is known about the earliest of these peoples, who probably hunted wild animals and also ate wild plants. Digging in Rock Creek Park, **archaeologists**, or scientists who study the past, have found stone weapons and cooking dishes made in about 2000 BCE.

By the late 1500s CE, when the first Europeans arrived in the area, the Potomac River region was home to Native American people called the Piscataway. They belonged to the Algonquian group of peoples, who lived in a huge area that stretched from the East Coast to the Rocky Mountains. The Piscataway were a farming people who lived in small villages and tended crops such as beans, corn, squash, and tobacco. They also used nets to catch fish in the waters of the Potomac and Anacostia Rivers. The Piscataway were often at war with the Algonquians' traditional enemies, the Iroquois, who lived farther north.

When the Europeans arrived, the Piscataway had been weakened by years of conflict with the Iroquois. They found it difficult to resist the new arrivals on their land. The Natives also suffered because they caught diseases carried by the Europeans. These diseases had not been present until the explorers and settlers came, so the Native Americans had little immunity to them. By the 1680s, nearly all the Piscataway in the area were gone. Those who had survived moved north to join their old rivals, the Iroquois.

European navigators began to explore the coastal waters near present-day Washington, DC, in the early 1600s. In 1608, John Smith, who had founded a settlement at Jamestown, Virginia, a year earlier, mapped the Potomac River as far inland as the Great Falls. Smith's map showed many Native American villages along the banks of the river and beyond.

Land for the colony of Maryland was given to George Calvert, the first Lord Baltimore.

The first European who lived in the area that is now Washington, DC, was an Englishman named Henry Fleete. In 1632, he built an outpost on the Potomac River. There he traded with the Native Americans, giving them European supplies and tools in exchange for furs. That same year, the English king granted a large area of land called the Maryland Colony to a nobleman named George Calvert,

or Lord Baltimore. This new colony included the area that was to become Washington, DC. Calvert died just five weeks before Maryland officially became a colony. He had hoped the new land would be useful for commercial purposes and also as a refuge for English Catholics like himself. Though he did not live to see it, both of these goals were accomplished. Maryland became a leading tobacco-exporting colony and a place where thousands of Catholic immigrants could

Standout Speech

In 1999, a poll of leading scholars of public speeches named Dr. Martin Luther King's "I Have a Dream" speech, delivered in Washington, DC, in 1963, as the best political speech of the twentieth century. The speech makes reference to the Declaration of Independence, the Emancipation Proclamation, and the United States Constitution.

practice their religion. The Maryland Act of Toleration in 1649 gave religious freedom to all Christians.

In 1634, Calvert's son Leonard—accompanied by "twenty gentlemen … and 300 laboring men"—landed at Chesapeake Bay. They divided the Maryland Colony into huge plantations, called manors. The plantations began growing tobacco, which was then a new and very profitable crop. These plantations made their owners very wealthy. At first the work was done by indentured servants, or people who work for a time to pay a debt, but they were soon replaced by slaves brought from Africa. By the end of the seventeenth century, historians believe that about every third person in the Maryland Colony was a slave.

The land along the Potomac River remained mostly farmland until the mid-to-late eighteenth century. The first town in the area, Georgetown, was founded in 1751. This port on the Potomac gave the tobacco growers an easy way to ship their crops to markets in Europe. Georgetown was the farthest point upstream that boats could reach on the river. The town grew rapidly and thrived as a busy trading area for those buying and selling goods from the Maryland Colony. In 1765, a building called the Old Stone House was built in Georgetown. Today, it remains the oldest unchanged building in Washington, DC.

A New Capital for a New Nation

In 1776, the thirteen colonies along the East Coast declared their independence from Great Britain. Colonists and some European allies fought against British troops and eventually won. The new country needed a capital—a place where its lawmakers could meet. For almost twenty-five years, though, the United States of America did not have a permanent capital. The nation's lawmakers could not agree on a location for a permanent capital. The government moved many times in those years. The Congress met in Philadelphia, Baltimore, and New York City. It also

Among the places to serve as the capital of the United States before the construction of Washington, DC, was Philadelphia. Carpenters' Hall housed the First Continental Congress in 1774.

The Native People

Native Americans have lived in the area that became Washington, DC, and the surrounding lands for thousands of years. The largest tribe in the region is called the Piscataway, also known as the Conoy. Several other tribes that are closely related to the Piscataway lived there as well, including the Nacotchtank, Pamunkey, Mattapanient, Nangemeick, and Tauxehent. In nearby Delaware, most Native Americans were part of the Lenape and Nanticoke tribes.

These tribes spoke Algonquian Piscataway, a **dialect**, or related version, of the Nanticoke language. They lived in villages on the banks of the Potomac River, but they were also present in the land that would become Maryland and Delaware. The tribes in this area relied on farming

A European explorer created this image of Native people fishing in the Potomac.

for much of their food, raising crops like corn, beans, squash, and tobacco. They also fished in the river and hunted small game such as deer, elk, wolves, turkeys, and beavers. Berries and nuts supplemented their diet as well. They generally lived in longhouses, long structures with arched roofs covered in bark, leaves, and grasses. Their villages were palisaded, or surrounded by large fences or walls for protection.

European settlers arrived in the area in the early seventeenth century. One of best-known explorers to reach the region and encounter Native Americans at this time was English explorer Captain John Smith. This early encounter with Smith was relatively peaceful. However, a few years later, a group of English settlers led by Henry Fleete attacked the Nacotchtank people. Conflict continued when Fleete was captured by the tribe shortly after. He was held captive for five years. Over time, the Native American population in the area shrank due to war with settlers and disease brought by the new arrivals. The surviving Native Americans moved, many to other parts of Maryland or beyond. Many from the Nacotchtank tribe merged with the Piscataway.

Though there are a small number of Native Americans descended from these tribes living in the area, there are currently no federally recognized tribes in Washington, DC. In Maryland, the Piscataway and Piscataway Conoy tribes are recognized by the state.

Spotlight on the Piscataway

The Piscataway was once one of the largest and most powerful tribes in the region around Washington, DC. Its members spoke a language called Algonquian Piscataway.

Distribution: Today, though their population is smaller, Piscataway people still live and celebrate their heritage in this area. Many live in Maryland. Some are members of groups such as the Cedarville Band of Piscataway Indians that work to educate and share Piscataway culture and traditions.

Homes: Like many Algonquian tribes, the Piscataway lived mostly in longhouses—large rectangular structures with barrel-shaped roofs covered in bark or animal skin. They lived in villages made up of several longhouses and surrounded by walls for protection.

Food: The Piscataway relied on farming more than other Native American tribes in the region. They grew corn, squash, pumpkins, melons, and beans. They hunted small animals and birds. Thanks to their location near the Potomac and Anacostia Rivers, many also fished and caught oysters and clams.

Clothing: Piscataway art was made with items from nature. Woven belts, moccasins, bags and baskets, and other items would be made from turtle shells; the hide from a fox, deer, or other small animal; or clam shells. Handmade tools were also important to the Piscataway's interaction with English settlers. In the early days of settlement, the relationship between the Native people and the English was fairly peaceful in this region. The Piscataway would trade tools and weapons with the settlers in exchange for metal goods, food, and other valuable items.

met in a number of smaller towns in Pennsylvania, Maryland, and New Jersey.

They finally turned to someone who was very respected—George Washington. General Washington had led colonial troops against the British and had become the nation's first president in 1789. One reason why Washington chose the site on the Potomac River was because it was located almost in the middle of all the new states that lined the Atlantic coast. Lawmakers could travel there easily no matter where they lived. The site was also very close to Washington's home in Virginia, so he knew the area well. Washington also decided that the capital should be in a separate district that was not part of any state.

Not everyone was enthusiastic about this location. Thomas Jefferson, who was Washington's secretary of state, said it was nothing more than "a swamp in the wilderness." Even with this objection, Congress decided in 1790 to build the capital here. They called the new capital Washington in the president's honor. The state of Maryland gave 70 square miles (181 sq km) of land, and Virginia gave another 30 square miles (78 sq km). This section of land was given the second part of its name, the District of Columbia, for the explorer Christopher Columbus.

George Washington called on Pierre Charles L'Enfant to design a city that would become the nation's capital. L'Enfant was a Frenchman who had come to fight on the side of the colonists during the Revolutionary War. After the war, he worked as an architect and engineer in New York. L'Enfant spent three weeks exploring the site Washington had chosen. He was helped by two brilliant assistants—Andrew Ellicott, a local surveyor, and Benjamin Banneker,

Pierre Charles L'Enfant designed Washington, DC, but was fired after complaints from residents.

an African American who was raised a freeman in Maryland. Banneker was mostly self educated. He assisted Ellicott as a surveyor, but he later became known as an astronomer and a writer.

In his plans, L'Enfant imagined that the Congress would meet in a grand building on Jenkins Hill—later renamed Capitol Hill. The president would live in a great mansion on Pennsylvania Avenue. Many wide streets and avenues would fan out from the hill, and buildings, monuments, and statues would be scattered all over the city.

L'Enfant's plan—and his hot temper—made him very unpopular with the local landowners. One of the landowners was building a house exactly where L'Enfant planned to put a street. L'Enfant had the house torn down. When he did this, the landowners demanded that L'Enfant be fired, which he was. When he left, L'Enfant took his plans with him. Benjamin Banneker was able to reconstruct the plans from memory.

Benjamin Banneker re-created plans for Washington, DC, from memory.

By 1800, the city of Washington was ready for the government to move in. However, only one wing of the Capitol was finished, along with a few other government buildings. The city's unpaved streets were choked with dust in dry weather, and a sea of mud when it rained. People dumped garbage in the streets, and pigs and cows wandered freely. The government did not need very much space in those days. In 1800, the government employed only 127 people.

On November 2, 1800, John Adams became the first president to live in Washington, DC. The White House was not finished when Adams moved in, though. The plaster on the walls was still wet in places, and many rooms were unfinished. Still, Adams remained enthusiastic about the White House, and wrote his wife, Abigail, that "none but honest and wise men [shall] ever rule under this roof." Abigail found the White House drafty and

Making a Soda Bottle Cherry Tree Blossom Painting

Visitors and residents have enjoyed the beauty of blossoming cherry trees in Washington, DC, since they were introduced to the city in the early twentieth century. Each year, this admiration for the cherry blossoms culminates in hundreds of thousands of people visiting the city for the annual National Cherry Blossom Festival. You can make your own cherry tree blossom painting by recycling an old soda bottle.

What You Need

Paper

Black and pink poster paint

Paintbrushes

Paper plates (2)

Empty 2-liter soda bottle

What To Do

- Ensure the bottom of the soda bottle is clean; wash and remove labels as needed.
- Pour some black paint onto one of the paper plates. Pour a larger amount of pink paint onto the other plate—enough to dip the bottom of the soda bottle in.
- Using the black paint and your paintbrush, paint the trunk and branches of your cherry tree on the paper. Cherry trees are usually not perfectly straight, so feel free to paint your trunk and branches in that way.
- Dip the bottom of the soda bottle into the pink paint. The five bumps on the bottom of the bottle should now be coated with the pink paint.
- Carefully press the bottom of the soda bottle onto your tree's branches so the pink "blossoms" are printed on them. Repeat for each branch.
- Allow your painting to dry completely before hanging or displaying. Don't forget to sign your painting!

cold, and she often hung laundry in the unfinished rooms. She called it "the great castle." They lived there for only five months before Thomas Jefferson defeated Adams in the 1800 presidential election.

Washington at War

The capital was still under construction when the new country went to war for the first time. The War of 1812 was fought against Britain, mostly over the right of ships to travel freely on the Atlantic Ocean. On August 24, 1814, the British forces attacked and burned much of Washington, DC, including the White House, the Capitol, and the bridge over the Potomac River. The Library of Congress, including the three thousand volumes it housed, was destroyed. President James Madison and his government were forced to flee to Maryland. The house where Madison stayed, owned by Caleb Bentley, is still known today as the Madison House. Only a sudden thunderstorm, which put out many of the fires, saved the city from complete destruction. The British quickly withdrew from the city rather than face a counterattack. Soon after, British troops lost a few key battles, and on December 24, 1814, the two sides signed a peace treaty and returned all conquered land to each other.

In the years after the War of 1812, Congress moved quickly to begin rebuilding the nation's capital. During this time, many of Washington's most familiar landmarks appeared. By the end of the 1820s, the White House had been rebuilt and the Capitol was nearly complete. In 1848, construction of the Washington Monument began. The first part of the Smithsonian Institution opened in 1852. This peaceful period of growth lasted only a few decades, though. In the early 1860s, war came to Washington, DC, again, largely because of an issue that had troubled the country since its beginning—slavery.

Washington, DC, was an important center of the slave trade. Slaves were auctioned off along the National Mall. By 1850, though, the abolitionist movement, which was trying to end slavery across the United States, succeeded in banning the slave trade in Washington, DC. Slavery still existed in the city, but buying and selling slaves was now illegal. By

In Their Own Words

Today all the city is in mourning, nearly every house being in black and I have not seen a smile, no business, and many a strong man I have seen in tears."
—Dr. George Brainard Todd, eyewitness to the Lincoln assassination

The British burned the new city of Washington, DC, near the end of the War of 1812.

1860, Washington, DC, was home to more than eleven thousand free blacks and more than three thousand slaves.

The slavery issue inflamed tensions between the South, where slavery was widely practiced, and the North, where it was mostly against the law. In 1861, the Southern states declared themselves independent, and the Civil War broke out.

A conflict in 1861 near Washington, DC, showed the divide in the country. The conflict was called the Baltimore Riot. On April 19, a group of soldiers from the Massachusetts Militia passed through Baltimore on their way to DC to join the Union forces. Many in Maryland were antiwar and sympathized with their Southern neighbors, and a group of these civilians surrounded the Massachusetts soldiers and attacked them. The troops fought back and soon the conflict escalated to a brawl in the streets of Baltimore. Four soldiers and twelve civilians were killed in the riot. Some historians consider Sumner Henry Needham, the first of the soldiers to be killed, to be the first Union casualty of the war.

At the beginning of the war, Washington, DC, had only one fort to protect it. When Major General George McClellan became responsible for the city's defense, he led an expansive buildup of entrenchments and forts covering 33 miles (53 km) of land around the district. He placed the forts on high hills to make them harder to reach. When the expansion was complete, Washington, DC, was considered one of the most heavily defended cities in the world.

The war between the Union (North) and the Confederacy (South) was long and difficult, and it came dangerously close to Washington, DC, which was part of the North. One of the first major battles of the war was fought at Manassas Junction, Virginia, on July 21, 1861, about 25 miles (40 km) outside of Washington, DC. The North lost that battle, better known as the First Battle of Bull Run, and thousands of wounded men streamed into the district.

Throughout the war, Washington's hospitals could not hold the sick and wounded who were filling the city. Many homes, churches, and government buildings, including parts of the Capitol, were used as hospital wards.

The Civil War also caused drastic changes to the city's water system. The water supply was severely strained by the large numbers of people who were now living there. As a result, the Army Corps of Engineers built a new **aqueduct,** or channel for carrying water, that eased the demand on the city's water supply.

African-American students were educated in segregated schools for many decades after the Civil War.

★ 10 ★ KEY MEMORIALS AND MONUMENTS

Arlington National Cemetery

Lincoln Memorial

Martin Luther King Jr. Memorial

1. African American Civil War Memorial and Museum

The African American Civil War Memorial and Museum honors and recognizes the soldiers who fought for freedom during the Civil War. The site includes a memorial wall that lists the names of these soldiers, and a museum.

2. Army National Military Cemeteries

Arlington National Cemetery in Arlington, Virginia, and the Soldiers' and Airmen's Home National Cemetery in Washington, DC, honor those who served our nation. The grounds of these cemeteries feature stone monuments to those who lost their lives protecting our country.

3. Franklin Delano Roosevelt Memorial

This unique memorial honors the legacy of our thirty-second president with four outdoor rooms to represent FDR's four terms in office. It also includes a statue of FDR's wife, Eleanor, the only presidential memorial to depict a first lady.

4. Korean War Veterans Memorial

The Korean War Veterans Memorial honors the 5.8 million Americans who fought during the three-year period of the Korean War (1950-1953). The memorial includes nineteen stainless steel statues representing a cross section of soldiers.

5. Lincoln Memorial

One of the most popular tourist attractions in Washington, DC, is this memorial dedicated to Abraham Lincoln. The space features thirty-six columns, representing the number of states in the Union at the time of Lincoln's death.

6. Martin Luther King Jr. Memorial

This memorial in West Potomac Park, dedicated in 2011, covers 4 acres (1.6 ha) and includes a 30-foot- (9 m) high granite statue of King. Visitors can also see the Inscription Wall, featuring fourteen quotes by King.

7. Thomas Jefferson Memorial

This memorial, dedicated to our third president, was built to give the impression the statue of Jefferson is gazing toward the White House. Like many other memorials in DC, the Jefferson Memorial is run by the National Park Service.

8. Ulysses S. Grant Memorial

This memorial depicts US president and Civil War general Grant sitting on horseback. The main part of the sculpture is 17 feet (5 m) tall, making it the second-largest equestrian statue in the United States. The statue faces the Lincoln Memorial.

9. Vietnam Veterans Memorial

The Vietnam Veterans Memorial is made up of the Three Servicemen Memorial statue, the Vietnam Women's Memorial, and the Memorial Wall. The Memorial Wall includes the names of more than fifty-eight thousand servicemen and women who gave their lives.

10. Washington Monument

The Washington Monument is four-sided and tapers to a pyramid-like shape at the top. In 2011, the monument was damaged by an earthquake and by Hurricane Irene, which struck Washington, DC. It reopened in 2014.

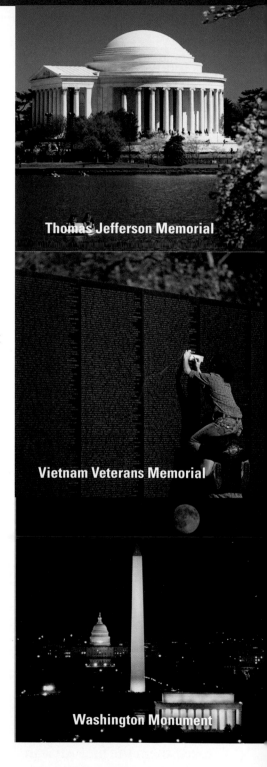

Thomas Jefferson Memorial

Vietnam Veterans Memorial

Washington Monument

On April 14, 1865, Washington, DC, was shocked by one of the most tragic events ever to take place there. Abraham Lincoln, who was president at the time, was assassinated, or killed, by John Wilkes Booth at Ford's Theatre on Tenth Street. Lincoln was watching a play called *Our American Cousin* at the time that he was shot by Booth, an actor who had sided with the South. Lincoln was carried to a house across the street and died there the next morning. He was the first American

president to be assassinated. The assassination occurred five days after the commander of the Confederate Army of Northern Virginia, General Robert E. Lee, surrendered to Lieutenant General Ulysses S. Grant and the Union Army of the Potomac. The surrender took place at Appomattox Court House, Virginia, about 145 miles (233 km) southwest of Washington, DC.

After his assassination, Lincoln's body was displayed at the Capitol rotunda in a ceremony called "lying in state." It was an opportunity for Americans to mourn their president. Thousands of citizens visited the nation's capital to pay their respects to President Lincoln.

The Civil War changed Washington, DC, and the country in many ways. The Confederate states were brought back into the Union and slavery was officially abolished throughout the country. Washington's population increased, growing from seventy-five thousand in 1860 to more than one hundred thousand in 1865. Many of these new Washingtonians were African Americans moving from the South. The free black people of Washington began to play an even more important role in the life of the city.

In the years after the war, a government agency called the Freedmen's Bureau founded schools for black people all over the city. The most famous of these schools is Howard University, which opened its doors in 1867. Today it is considered one of the top historically black colleges or universities in the country. African Americans also began to play a role in Washington, DC, politics. In 1868, two black men were elected to the city council. This made them the first African Americans ever to hold political office in the city.

In 1871, Washington, DC, was officially declared a **municipal** corporation. This meant that the city (including Georgetown) was combined with the county of Washington and the District of Columbia to form a single unit. In 1874, after financial problems left the city deeply in debt, Congress decided that Washingtonians would no longer have the right to run their own city. Instead of an elected government, Washington was to be managed by three people appointed by the president. One reason for this decision was that some Southern leaders in Congress, who opposed equal rights for African Americans, did not want to see black people gain political power in the nation's capital. Another reason was that some of Washington's elected officials were not wisely using the district's money.

Modern Washington

When the twentieth century began, Washington, DC, was well on its way to becoming one of the world's great cities. The federal government had grown so much that it now employed more than 25,000 workers. In 1917, the United States entered World War I. During the war, the government needed more workers. This helped Washington's population to grow, reaching 450,000. During this period and into the 1920s, a great deal of construction was done in Washington, DC. The Lincoln Memorial was finished in 1922.

Many things had changed in Washington, DC, but some, such as the economic conditions of the city's black residents, did not. African Americans could enter most public places and ride freely on the city's streetcars. However, jobs and other forms of opportunity were not open to blacks. This was made worse

Men were forced to sell apples as Washington, DC, suffered with the rest of the country during the Great Depression.

in 1929 when the Great Depression hit. During the Depression, the country's economy collapsed. Millions of people all over the country lost their jobs. Many of them poured into Washington, DC, looking for work. At one point in 1934, almost forty thousand people were arriving in the city every day! In all parts of the country, businesses closed and farms were abandoned. Many people left their homes and moved westward, looking for more opportunities.

Some relief came when President Franklin D. Roosevelt's government created "make-work projects." These projects were designed to give jobs to unemployed people, while also improving the country. Workers repaired roads and bridges all across the country. In the west, many workers were sent to lumber camps to cut down trees. Many of Washington's great buildings, including the Supreme Court Building and the Jefferson Memorial, were completed during the 1930s, putting many unemployed people to work.

The United States entered World War II in 1941, sending soldiers to help fight against Japanese, German, and Italian troops. The war improved the nation's economy. In Washington, DC, more government workers were hired. Factories and farms across the country reopened to produce supplies for the war effort.

Bethesda, northwest of Washington, DC, is one of the nation's wealthiest suburbs.

After the war, things in the district began to change once again. Many of the white residents living in the district began to move to the surrounding suburbs. They still worked in Washington, DC, but they lived in homes that were 15 miles (24 km) or more away. At the same time, more and more African Americans were moving up from the South. The result was that, by 1960, the population of Washington, DC, was 54 percent African American.

Monumental Embarrassment

In 1853, the Washington Monument was in the middle of construction when the Washington National Monument Society ran out of funds. For more than two decades, the monument sat unfinished. Building did not begin again until after the end of the Civil War. The monument was completed in 1885.

The District of Columbia, at that time, had a bigger population than many states. Yet it still had no voice in its own political affairs. In 1960, Congress changed this situation slightly, when it approved the Twenty-Third Amendment to the US Constitution. This amendment finally gave the residents of Washington, DC, the right to vote in presidential elections.

The 1960s were a time when black people all over the country were demanding to be treated like all other Americans. Across the country, African Americans were often treated differently from white people. They were not allowed the same rights as white people. For example, special areas were set aside in restaurants for blacks only, and African Americans were forced to ride at the back of city buses and give up their seats to white people. African-American children were forced to go to all-black schools, which were almost never as good as the all-white schools. The civil rights movement had developed to fight these inequalities. The movement had one of its most historic moments in Washington, DC, on August 28, 1963. More than two hundred thousand people of many races marched to the steps of the Lincoln Memorial to hear the Reverend Martin Luther King Jr. give his famous "I Have a Dream" speech.

On April 4, 1968, King was assassinated in Memphis, Tennessee, which was a great blow to the civil rights movement. In the days that followed, many Americans were angry, and a number of America's cities, including Washington, DC, were torn apart by terrible riots. Large sections of Washington, DC, were destroyed by fire and looting. Nine people were killed, and hundreds more were injured. The areas rebuilt slowly, but some were never the same again. Eventually, African Americans and other minorities were given

A quarter of a million people heard Martin Luther King Jr. give his "I Have a Dream" speech in the district in 1963.

more equal rights. However, racial equality remained an important issue in many of Washington's neighborhoods.

Beginning in the early 1970s, Washingtonians gained more influence in government. In 1970, they were allowed to elect one nonvoting member to the House of Representatives. This special member could speak in debates and attend hearings, but could not vote for or against laws.

In 1973, Congress finally allowed Washingtonians to elect their own

city government. At the time, the city, like many other cities across the country, was in serious trouble. Many of the city's residents moved away to the suburbs. Poverty was still widespread in the district, and so were drugs and violence. By the 1980s, gang activity

A plane crashed into the Pentagon during the terrorist attacks on September 11, 2001.

Baby Pandas

The National Zoo has been home to pandas since the early 1970s. Occasionally, a baby panda is born at the zoo, an event that captures the attention of animal lovers around the world. A baby named Tai Shan was born in 2005, Bao Bao was born in 2013, and Bei Bei was born in 2015.

had made Washington, DC, one of America's most dangerous cities, with one of the highest murder rates in the country. Several laws and programs were established to fight these problems, and some success has been made. Washington, DC, is still rebuilding and trying to improve the lives of its residents.

Washington, DC, has been affected by world events, as well, and the results have sometimes been very painful. On September 11, 2001, an airplane that was hijacked by terrorists crashed into the Pentagon—the huge military headquarters across the Potomac River. More than 180 people died in the aircraft and on the ground. The district grieved for the losses and slowly rebuilt the Pentagon.

After the attack on the Pentagon, the number of people visiting the city fell. However, in the more than ten years since, the tourism industry and the city as a whole have recovered.

★ 10 KEY DATES IN DISTRICT HISTORY

 1. From 11,000 BCE

Paleo-Indians live in the area around the Potomac River.

 2. June 30, 1632

The area that would become the Maryland Colony, including modern-day Washington, DC, is granted by Charles I to Sir George Calvert, otherwise known as Lord Baltimore.

 3. August 24, 1814

British soldiers overrun the inexperienced US militia defending Washington during the War of 1812. The British burn large sections of the city, including the White House.

 4. April 14, 1865

During a performance of the play *Our American Cousin*, actor John Wilkes Booth shoots President Abraham Lincoln at Washington's Ford's Theatre. Lincoln dies the next morning.

 5. October 9, 1888

The Washington Monument, the tallest structure in Washington, DC, is completed and opened to visitors, more than forty years after the cornerstone had been laid.

 6. March 29, 1961

The Twenty-Third Amendment is ratified, giving residents of Washington, DC, the right to vote in presidential elections through representation in the Electoral College.

 7. August 28, 1963

Martin Luther King Jr. delivers his "I Have a Dream" speech during the March on Washington for Jobs and Freedom.

 8. September 11, 2001

A plane hijacked by terrorists crashes into the Pentagon, killing more than 180 people. Other hijacked planes hit New York City and Pennsylvania.

 9. August 22, 2011

The Martin Luther King Jr. Memorial is unveiled to the public, the first statue honoring an African American to be constructed on the National Mall.

 10. September 16, 2013

Aaron Alexis opens fire at the headquarters of the Naval Seal Systems Command in the Washington Navy Yard, killing twelve people and injuring three.

TRUE REFORMER BUILDING

The U Street Corridor was known as Black Broadway because it attracted so many top African-American performers.

The People

For the first 150 years of its existence, Washington's population grew steadily. In 1800, the nation's new capital had just 14,093 residents. Today, more than 600,000 people call the district home. It has the twenty-fourth-largest population of any city in the United States.

These statistics do not give the whole picture, though. At many points over the last sixty years, Washington, DC, unlike many American cities, has actually been losing people. In 1950, the census showed a population of 802,178. Just ten years later, only 763,956 people lived in the district.

This was a trend that was happening all over the United States, as people moved to the suburbs, seeking better housing and better schools for their children. Few US cities, though, have been hit as hard by this "**reverse migration**" (people moving out of the city) as Washington, DC. The city's population continued to fall between 1990 and 2000, dropping 5.7 percent. This steady "people drain" caused many problems for the city, such as fewer taxes paid, which meant less money for schools, police departments, and other services. Things are looking up for Washington, DC, though. The 2010 census recorded a population growth of nearly thirty thousand people. Though recent polls show that growth has slowed a bit, residents remain hopeful that people will continue choosing to live and work in Washington, DC.

Who Are the Washingtonians?

In some ways, Washington, DC, is very different from most cities in the United States. One key difference is the size and importance of the city's African-American community. In 1960, Washington, DC, became the first city in the United States to have a majority black population. Today, African Americans make up a little more than 50 percent of the city's population. This is very different from the United States as a whole, which is 77.9 percent white and just 13.1 percent black.

Washington's black community has a long, proud history. Many of the most distinguished African Americans throughout history have lived in Washington, DC. These people include great writers such as Langston Hughes, musicians like Duke Ellington, civil rights leaders including Frederick Douglass, and Benjamin Oliver Davis, the first African American to become a general in the US Army. Washington's black community is very proud of its contribution to the city's history and culture. One of the parts of the Smithsonian Institution, the Anacostia Museum, is dedicated to celebrating African-American history and culture. The Frederick Douglass National Historic Site is another

A loss of population has reduced funding for schools in Washington, DC.

important place to learn about the city's African-American heritage. Douglass was the first African American to buy a house in the Old Anacostia neighborhood. The U Street Corridor is also known as "Black Broadway" because of its legacy of hosting black musicians such as Ellington, Pearl Bailey, and Cab Calloway. Other African-American landmarks in the city include the Thurgood Marshall Center for Service and Heritage, the African-American Civil War Museum, and Howard University, one of the nation's top historically black colleges.

Many of the district's neighborhoods are filled with elegant older homes.

The story of Washington, DC, is not just about black and white, however. The city also has a large Spanish-speaking, or Hispanic, community, mostly centered in the Adams Morgan neighborhood in Northwest DC. Hispanics make up about 10 percent of the city's population today. Many of the members of Washington's Hispanic community are recent immigrants from Central America, especially the nation of El Salvador. There are also significant numbers of Hispanic residents from Mexico, Guatemala, the Dominican Republic, Argentina, Chile, and Ecuador. Recent research has shown that despite the fact that **gentrification**—changes to a neighborhood that make it more expensive to live there—has forced some residents to move out of traditionally Hispanic neighborhoods, the overall Hispanic population in Washington, DC, is on the rise. According to the US census, the Hispanic population in Washington, DC, grew over 21 percent between 2000 and 2010. In 2010, Hispanics comprised 9.1 percent of the total population there.

There is also a small but vibrant Asian-American community in Washington, DC. This community is concentrated around Chinatown, in the Northwest section of the district. It represents slightly less than 4 percent of the city's population. Between 2000 and 2010, the Asian population in Washington, DC, grew by about 60 percent. Hundreds of thousands more Asian Americans live in the suburbs across the Potomac River. Just because the neighborhood is called Chinatown does not mean that only Chinese Americans live and

Cory Booker

Connie Chung

Alyson Hannigan

1. Cory Booker

Cory Booker is a New Jersey senator. Born in Washington, DC, in 1969, Booker attended Yale Law School. He is known for his commitment to New Jersey and his use of Twitter to communicate with the people he serves.

2. Connie Chung

Connie Chung was the first Asian American to host a nightly network television news program in the United States. She was born in Washington, DC, in 1946. She has worked for networks including ABC, CBS, NBC, and CNN.

3. Duke Ellington

Many people consider Edward Kennedy "Duke" Ellington one of the most important musicians in American history. He was born in 1899, in Washington. The Duke Ellington Orchestra played concerts all over the world until Ellington's death in 1974.

4. Alyson Hannigan

Born in Washington, DC, in 1974, Alyson Hannigan is an actress best known for her roles on television. Her notable characters include Willow on the series *Buffy the Vampire Slayer* and Lily in *How I Met Your Mother*.

5. Taraji P. Henson

Actress Taraji P. Henson was born in Washington, DC, in 1970 and attended Howard University. She has appeared in a number of successful films and television shows, including *The Curious Case of Benjamin Button* and *Empire*.

6. J. Edgar Hoover

John Edgar Hoover was born in DC in 1895. In 1924, he became the director of the federal government's Bureau of Investigation—later renamed the Federal Bureau of Investigation (FBI). He became famous for tracking down gangsters and bank robbers.

7. Sugar Ray Leonard

Sugar Ray Leonard is considered one of the greatest boxers ever. He was born in North Carolina but his family moved to Washington, DC, when he was three. He won thirty-six matches and lost only three during his professional career.

8. Bill Nye

Scientist Bill Nye "the Science Guy" was born in 1955 in Washington, DC. Nye has appeared on many television shows and written several books. Recently, he worked on the Mars Exploration Rover missions.

9. Norah O'Donnell

Norah O'Donnell, the co-anchor of *CBS This Morning*, was born in Washington, DC, in 1974. She graduated from Georgetown University before beginning her career as a journalist. She has served as a reporter for the *Today Show*, *NBC Nightly News*, and *MSNBC*.

10. John Philip Sousa

This bandleader and composer, known as the March King, was born in Washington, DC, in 1854. John Philip Sousa wrote many patriotic compositions, including "Semper Fidelis," the official march of the US Marines, and "The Stars and Stripes Forever."

J. Edgar Hoover

Bill Nye

Norah O'Donnell

Who Washingtonians Are

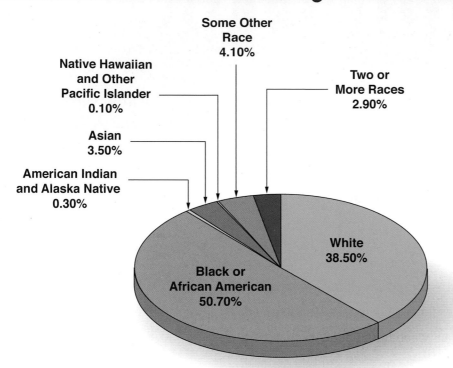

Some Other Race
4.10%

Native Hawaiian and Other Pacific Islander
0.10%

Asian
3.50%

American Indian and Alaska Native
0.30%

Two or More Races
2.90%

White
38.50%

Black or African American
50.70%

Total Population 601,723

Hispanic or Latino (of any race):
• 54,749 people (9.1%)

Note: The pie chart shows the racial breakdown of the state's population based on the categories used by the US Bureau of the Census. The Census Bureau reports information for Hispanics or Latinos separately, since they may be of any race. Percentages in the pie chart may not add to 100 because of rounding.

Source: US Bureau of the Census, 2010 Census

work there. The city's Asian population comes from many other places, too, including Vietnam, Japan, and other countries in Southeast Asia. People from India have become the largest and fastest-growing group in the area.

The greater Washington area is one of the country's most important destinations for immigrants. During the 1990s, almost 250,000 people from other countries came to live in the area. Only about 13 percent of them chose to live in the district itself. Most immigrants moved to the suburbs. The largest concentration of immigrants in the district is in the Adams Morgan neighborhood, where almost 25 percent of all residents were born outside the United States. Immigrants from all over the world make the Adams Morgan neighborhood one of Washington's most colorful and interesting communities. People from as far away as Ethiopia and Peru have opened shops and restaurants in the area. Adams Morgan's main street, Columbia Road, offers some of the best ethnic food in the city. Many immigrants move to Washington, DC, to find new job opportunities and make better lives for their families. The area's great number of information technology companies and other high-tech industries attract many people from foreign countries.

Washington, DC, sometimes seems like the crossroads of the world. Take a walk along the Mall—or down Massachusetts Avenue or near Dupont Circle—and you may hear a

The Asian population of Washington, DC, has been growing rapidly.

dozen different languages being spoken. This is because the district has a very large number of foreign-born people. Many are immigrants, but thousands more are temporary visitors. They work for their countries' embassies or for international organizations with offices in the city. Still others are students at Washington's colleges and universities. Many of these people will return to their own countries someday, but some will also make Washington, DC, their permanent home.

Immigrants play an important role in Washington's economy. In 2010, about 18 percent of all business owners in the city were foreign-born. Research published in 2013 showed they comprised nearly 17 percent of the district's workforce.

Things to See and Do in Washington

Wherever they come from, Washingtonians love to take advantage of the pleasures the city has to offer. These include cultural activities, ranging from opera and ballet at the Kennedy Center to jazz and blues at the famous Blues Alley club in Georgetown. Many of the district's fine museums attract both residents and visitors. The Museum of Natural History is the place to learn about the past and present state of our natural world— from dinosaur skeletons to currently endangered species. The National Air and Space Museum offers the opportunity to discover facts about space travel, the solar system, and the innovation that made it possible to explore outer space. There you can see the first powered airplane flown by the Wright brothers, the Apollo 11 command module, and even a rock from the moon. Visitors to the Bureau of Engraving and Printing can see real money being printed, and the Washington Navy Yard offers interactive exhibits and displays to learn about the history of the US Navy.

Washingtonians love to enjoy the outdoors, especially during warm weather. A warm summer day might find Washington's residents rowing a rented boat on the Tidal Basin, shooting a basketball on an outdoor court, or enjoying a brass-band concert on the Mall. Residents and visitors love to stroll through Rock Creek Park, which has large areas that

Taking Flight

The National Air and Space Museum is home to impressive artifacts that include some of our nation's greatest achievements in science and technology. However, the museum itself started in a much simpler way—with a small collection of kites. The Smithsonian Institution acquired the kites from the Chinese Imperial Commission in 1876.

feel almost like wilderness regions. Rock Creek Park has over 32 miles (51.5 km) of trails for walking, jogging or biking. The park also features plenty of picnic areas, a tennis center, horse-riding trails, and areas to golf and boat. Rock Creek Park even has its own planetarium that offers weekly free astronomy programs led by park rangers. Another favorite outdoor spot is the Chesapeake & Ohio Canal National Historic Park. This is a nineteenth-century canal along which people can walk or ride bicycles. They can even ride on barges pulled by mules, just like in the old days. The C&O Canal was designated as a national monument in 1961 and as a national park in 1971. The park's diverse terrain makes it an ideal place for running, hiking, biking, fishing, boating kayaking, and camping. In 1996, heavy rains following a blizzard in January caused significant flooding and damage to the canal and park, but officials and volunteers restored the area to its original state. Another great outdoor spot is the Smithsonian National Zoological Park, one of the country's best zoos. It is home to more than two thousand animals. The zoo's most famous residents are the giant pandas from China. Asian elephants, exotic birds, and big cats like lions and tigers also have a home at the National Zoo. One of the most loved features is the O Line, an overhead system of cables that allows the zoo's orangutans to travel between two parts of the ape exhibit—over the heads of visitors! For those who are unable to visit the zoo in person, camera feeds of many exhibits can be viewed online.

Some people say the only thing Washingtonians love more than politics is sports. One of the most popular sports in the city is basketball, whether it is played in a schoolyard or by the Georgetown University team. Washington, DC, has professional basketball, football, and hockey teams. The Washington Wizards, part of the National Basketball Association, have played under that name since 1997, but have existed as the region's professional basketball team since the 1960s. They were formerly known as the Baltimore Bullets, the Capital Bullets, and the Washington Bullets. They play at the Verizon Center, as do the Washington Capitals, the city's professional hockey team, and the Washington Mystics of the WNBA. The

The Washington Nationals entertain fans of all ages in a new stadium in Anacostia.

Capitals were founded in the 1974 season. Washingtonians were overjoyed in 2005 when a new team, the Nationals, brought Major League Baseball to the city for the first time in more than thirty years. The team plays at Nationals Park near the Anacostia River. This was not the first time Washington, DC, had a professional baseball team, however. The Washington Senators played in the city from 1901 to 1960 before moving to Minnesota. The city was granted an expansion franchise in 1961, but that team moved to Dallas-Fort Worth in 1972.

Washington's team in the National Football League has a strong fan base among city residents, and it has won three Super Bowls. However, it has been a source of controversy in recent years. The team's name is the Washington Redskins, a name that many consider offensive and hurtful to Native Americans. Many Native American tribes and advocacy groups officially oppose the name of the team and have asked that it be changed. Many other people have made the same statement, including public officials, sports commentators, and journalists. In 2014, the United States Patent and Trademark Office voted to cancel the team's federal trademark because it considered it offensive to Native Americans. However, many fans say the name is a tradition and not intended to be hurtful. The team's owner, Daniel Snyder, has said he has no plans to change the name.

With its diverse population and interesting sites and events—from museums and festivals to the countless outdoor activities—Washington, DC, has a lot to offer everyone.

10 KEY EVENTS

Arlington Cemetery Memorial Day Ceremony

Cherry Blossom Festival

1. Arlington Cemetery Memorial Day Ceremony

Each Memorial Day, Washington residents and visitors honor the fallen soldiers buried in Arlington National Cemetery. Wreaths are placed at the grave of John F. Kennedy and the Tomb of the Unknown Soldier, and the president often gives a speech.

2. Blossom Kite Festival

Every April, the skies around the Washington Monument fill with kites. Children of all ages take kite-making classes and compete for prizes. The high point of the festival is the Rokkaku Battle, a battle among Japanese-style fighting kites.

3. Boo at the Zoo

Every October, visitors to the National Zoo can have a spooky good time with their animal friends. Boo at the Zoo features treat stations for costumed trick-or-treaters, as well as live demonstrations with the zoo's animals and decorated trails to explore.

4. Cherry Blossom Festival

This annual event happens in March or April, when pink and white flowers begin to appear on the Japanese cherry trees in West Potomac. The festival celebrates the close ties between the American and Japanese people.

5. Chinese New Year Parade

During the Chinese New Year, in January or February, the streets of Chinatown come alive with dancers and exploding firecrackers. Other Chinese New Year celebrations include live music performances and eating traditional Chinese food.

WASHINGTON, DC

6. DC Caribbean Carnival

Every June, the members of Washington's West Indian community throw a lively and colorful street party in the city. There is traditional music and a huge parade of spectacular floats and costumes. Food, crafts, and arts are also featured.

7. National Christmas Tree Lighting

This ceremony has been a holiday tradition since 1923. Every year, thousands of people are delighted when a Christmas tree is lit up in the Ellipse, a park near the White House. Celebrity hosts, performers, and the first family highlight this televised affair.

8. National Independence Day Celebration

Washington, DC, celebrates America's birthday in grand style, with a parade along Constitution Avenue, a concert on the Capitol steps, and a huge display of fireworks at the Washington Monument.

9. Smithsonian Folklife Festival

This event, held in June and July, showcases traditional arts and cultures. As you walk down the National Mall, you might hear a bluegrass band from Kentucky, see multicultural crafts, or taste delicious food.

10. White House Easter Egg Roll

Children have been rolling brightly colored Easter eggs across the White House lawn since 1878, when President Rutherford B. Hayes began the tradition. This favorite Washington event, which includes live music, games, and entertainment, happens on Easter Monday.

Independence Day

White House Easter Egg Roll

The Council of the District of
Columbia meets in this building
on Pennsylvania Avenue.

How the Government Works

Washington, DC, has a system of government that is unlike that of any other place in the United States. The district is the home of the federal government—as well as home to many of the most powerful people in the country—but it also has its own government. The district's government, however, does not function like the government of other cities or states. This is—at least partly—the way the nation's founders wanted it. They feared that the people of Washington, DC, would be able to control the federal government if the city had too much power. In the process, though, they also limited the power Washingtonians have over their own city's affairs.

For almost a century, Washington had no municipal, or city, government at all. Between 1874 and 1973, the District of Columbia was managed by a congressional committee. This committee—which was appointed, not elected—usually neglected the city. Washington seldom received enough money to build modern schools and hospitals or to keep its roads and bridges in good condition.

Even after the district regained the right to elect its own municipal government, it still lacked some of the basic powers that almost every other city in the United States has. The most important is the ability to raise money. Most cities pay for the things they need

Congress meets in Washington, DC, but the city's residents have no full members in either the House of Representatives or the Senate.

through taxes. The people who live or work in a city pay many taxes on their earnings or on the property they own. The taxes are used to pay for things the district needs. Washington's ability to make people pay taxes, though, is very limited. In most cities, property taxes are the most important source of government funds. In Washington, nearly 60 percent of all property cannot be taxed. This is because it belongs either to the federal government or to foreign countries.

Citizens of Washington, DC, also have a different kind of representation in the federal government. Because it is not a traditional state, DC does not have true voting representation in Congress. The district is represented by a delegate in the US House of Representatives who is only allowed to vote on procedural matters and in congressional committees. Washington, DC, has no representation in the US Senate. In 1961, the Twenty-Third Amendment granted the district three electoral votes in presidential elections. This lack of power has been frustrating for Washington, DC, residents since the city's earliest days. Many use the phrase "taxation without representation" in protest of this situation—meaning residents pay taxes but do not see the benefit of them like other states. In fact, some Washington, DC, car license plates have the phrase "taxation without

WASHINGTON, DC

DZ ☰★★★ 1555

TAXATION WITHOUT REPRESENTATION

SEE WINDOW STICKER

SEE WINDOW STICKER

representation" on them. In 2013, President Barack Obama made a statement in favor of DC voting rights by using these license plates on the presidential limousine.

Another problem is that many of the people who work in the district are commuters who live elsewhere. In other large cities where people live in suburbs and commute into the city—such as in New York City—the state makes commuters pay a portion of their income in taxes to the city where they earn their living. Federal law does not allow Washington to do this, which puts a greater burden on the people who do live and pay taxes in Washington, DC. Property taxes and income tax are much higher in the district than in the surrounding suburbs. This is one of the main reasons so many people choose to live in Virginia or Maryland and commute to their jobs in Washington.

Washington, DC, also has very limited control over how it can spend the money it raises. In 1995, after the city found itself deep in debt and unable to pay many of its bills, Congress created a control board to oversee Washington's financial decisions. This board, whose members are appointed rather than elected, had to give its approval before the city could spend money on new projects. In 2001, Washington, DC, had a balanced budget for the fourth year in a row, and the control board suspended its activities.

Silly Law

It is against the law in Washington, DC, to take photographs in public for more than five minutes at a time. The law was intended to apply to professional street photographers and is rarely enforced, so tourists can feel free to keep snapping photos.

Local government in Washington, DC, is unique as it functions as a city but also must provide some services to citizens like a state. The city's government is divided into executive, judicial and legislative branches.

Branches of Government

Executive

This branch of government is responsible for the day-to-day management of the city. It is headed by the mayor, who is elected to a four-year term by all the voters of the city. A mayor can serve an unlimited number of terms. The mayor appoints people to run the police and fire departments, the school system, and other parts of the city government. One unique aspect of the DC mayoral office is that the mayor has no official residence, or house, to live in during his or her time as mayor. In 2001, the city council approved plans to purchase land and a building to be used as a residence for the mayor, but after many arguments about the location and use of the land, the plans were abandoned.

Legislative

The Council of the District of Columbia votes on proposals for things that the city might choose to do, such as raising property taxes or building new schools. There are thirteen members of the council. One is elected by the voters in each of the city's eight electoral districts, and five more are elected by all of the city's voters. To be eligible for a seat on the council, a candidate must have lived in Washington, DC, for at least one year prior to the general election, be a registered voter, and hold no other public office for which they are paid. Some residents have concerns that because there are only thirteen members, and it therefore only takes seven votes to pass legislation, it is too easy for the council to be swayed one way or another. Still, others say the streamlined council is more efficient than larger governing bodies in other states.

Judicial

Washington's judicial, or court, system has two levels: the Superior Court and the Court of Appeals. The Superior Court, which has one chief judge, sixty-one associate judges, and twenty-four magistrate judges, handles most criminal and civil cases. These range from trials for crimes such as murder and drug trafficking to tax disputes. The Court of Appeals, with one chief judge and eight associate judges, has the power to review any decision made by the lower court. The president appoints all of the judges for fifteen-year terms. There are no limits on the number of terms a judge can serve.

A statue of Abraham Lincoln stands outside the Superior Courthouse in the district.

Making Your Voice Heard

If you live in Washington, DC, the federal government is practically next door. You can tour the White House and the Capitol, sit in on congressional hearings, and see almost every part of your federal government in action. Even though Washingtonians do not have a direct say in how the federal government is run, they can still make their voices heard. You also have a say in your municipal government.

The best way to begin is by learning as much as you can about the important issues facing the district. Washington's daily newspapers, radio and television stations, and the Internet are very good sources of information about politics in the district. Once you have learned everything you can about the issues, contact your federal and municipal representatives by telephone, mail, or e-mail, and let them know what you think. You can make a difference!

Population Explosion

Most of the people who work in Washington, DC, commute to the district from the surrounding suburbs. In fact, according to the 2010 US census, the daytime population of DC is nearly double the amount of people who really live there—an increase of 79 percent during the day.

POLITICAL FIGURES
FROM WASHINGTON, DC

Muriel Bowser: Mayor, 2015-

Muriel Bowser is the second woman to be elected mayor of Washington, DC. Previously, she represented DC's Ward 4 on the Council of the District of Columbia and was a member of the council's Advisory Neighborhood Commission. She is a graduate of American University.

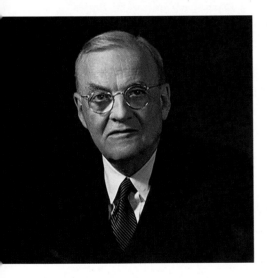

John Foster Dulles: Secretary of State, 1953-1959

An attorney and diplomat, John Foster Dulles helped form the United Nations in the 1940s and was appointed a US senator for New York State in 1949 but lost in the next election. President Dwight Eisenhower appointed him secretary of state, a post he left shortly before he died in May 1959. Dulles International Airport was named in his honor after his death.

Anthony A. Williams: Mayor, 1999-2007

Anthony Williams had a long career in politics before becoming Washington's fifth mayor. He previously served as the district's chief financial officer and balanced the budget within his first two years in that post. During his mayoral career, he oversaw great growth and brought $40 billion of investment to the city.

WASHINGTON, DC
YOU CAN MAKE A DIFFERENCE

Contacting Lawmakers

If you are interested in contacting members of the Council of the District of Columbia, go to: **dccouncil.us**. There you can find out more about members of the council and legislative business.

Citizens Blazing Way for Bicyclists

Washington, DC, is known as a hard city for driving, with heavy traffic and long commutes. In 2013, citizens worked to make a difference for those who use a more environment-friendly form of transportation by showing their support for the Bicycle Safety Amendment Act. The act improved safety and protections for bicyclists in a number of ways. It allowed bike riders to get the same head start on cars that pedestrians do when crossing the street at an intersection. This makes it easier for drivers to see them. Additionally, it now requires organizers of events to obtain permits before they can block bike lanes, paths, or sidewalks. It modified an earlier law that required bikes to have a bell, instead simply requiring that all cyclists can make a warning noise with a bell, mechanical device, or their voice.

Bicycle advocacy groups such as the Washington Area Bicycling Association helped the bill get passed by contacting the DC council and mayor's office to voice their support, and by sharing their opinions about it in public and in the press. Thanks in part to these efforts, the council and mayor passed the act in October 2013, and it officially went into effect in January 2014.

A capsule from a *Gemini* spacecraft is one of the many artifacts that attract visitors to the Smithsonian's Air and Space Museum.

Making a Living

People who live in Washington, DC, sometimes call it a "**company town**." A company town is a place that centers around a single industry. The most important business in Washington, DC, is the United States government.

About 733,000 people work in the District of Columbia. About one-third of them have government jobs. The US government was the reason Washington, DC, was created, and it is still the most important element of life in the city. The people who work for the government do an amazing variety of jobs, from sending out tax refunds at the Internal Revenue Service to examining fingerprint evidence at the FBI crime laboratory. You can see some government employees at work by taking tours of government buildings. One of the more interesting tours is the one through the Bureau of Engraving and Printing in the Treasury Building, where dollar bills are printed at a rate of eight thousand sheets per minute. The Library of Congress is another good place to visit. This is the largest library in the world, with more than thirty-five million books and other printed materials. You can also tour the Library of Congress's Music Division to see valuable materials related to music and the performing arts, including rare instruments such as Stradivarius violins. The US Capitol building is another interesting spot to visit. Exhibition Hall in the Capitol tells the story of the United States Congress through artifacts, rare documents, videos, and more.

Many service workers are required to keep Washington's attractions ready for tourists.

Anyone who performs a service, rather than making a product, is a service worker. People who work for the government are part of the service industry. Service workers also include doctors, lawyers, teachers, and postal workers. Maintenance workers who provide services that help maintain the district and its sites are also service workers.

Many people in Washington, DC, work for the tourism industry. An estimated twenty million visitors come to Washington, DC, every year, either as tourists or on business. Visitors to the district take tours of government buildings, admire the monuments and statues in the city's parks, visit the museums, and attend musical performances. The district's hotels, restaurants, shops, and transportation businesses (such as taxi companies) provide employment for many Washington, DC, residents and draw in billions of dollars in revenue. According to the tourism group Destination DC, travel and tourism spending supports over seventy-four thousand jobs in the city annually.

The arts are an important part of the district. Washington, DC, draws art lovers from all over the world. The National Gallery of Art and the Hirshhorn Museum and Sculpture Garden have paintings and sculptures from every period and every style. The Smithsonian American Art Museum offers two locations dedicated to displaying the best works by artists from the United States. The National Museum of African Art is home to exhibits, collections, events, and educational opportunities showcasing the work of African artists, from ancient to modern times. At the Corcoran Gallery of Art, in addition to viewing the gallery's beautiful collection, visitors can sign up for youth or adult art classes. There is no shortage of performing arts, either. The Kennedy Center offers performances by symphony orchestras, opera and ballet companies, and jazz musicians. Washington, DC, has a lively theater scene, too. The district has the nation's second-highest number of **per capita** (per person) theater productions annually, second only to New York City. Washington, DC, is home to the National Theatre, also called "the theater of presidents" because it is located so close to the White House. It has operated longer than any other major touring house in the United States and has been rebuilt six times on the same location since it was founded in 1835. Many smaller regional theaters in Washington, DC, have a strong following as well. One of these theaters, the Woolly Mammoth Theatre Company, was one of the first in the country to offer "pay what you can" shows to make the performing arts available to audiences from diverse economic backgrounds.

The tourism industry provides jobs for many Washingtonians, such as hotel desk clerks, waiters, travel agents, park rangers, and museum guides. Without them, Washington's attractions could not function.

Transportation

An outstanding transportation network carries travelers to, from, and around Washington, DC. The city has one of the world's best subway systems, and the second busiest in the United States. The Metro carries more than eight hundred thousand riders on a typical day.

The Metro is one of the nation's busiest rapid transit systems.

★ 10 KEY★ INDUSTRIES

Currency

Education

1. Communications and Media

DC is one of the world's great communications centers. Many important newspapers and magazines are published in the district. In recent years, the DC area has become a leader in "new media," or online news outlets.

2. Currency

Washington's Bureau of Engraving and Printing develops and prints billions of dollars every year, to be delivered to the Federal Reserve System. The US Mint, which makes the country's coins, is also headquartered in Washington, DC.

3. Education

Washington has many colleges and universities. Well-known DC schools include Howard University, George Washington University, Georgetown University (bottom left), and American University. Thousands of students attend colleges or universities in the district, bringing more than $200 million a year into the local economy.

4. Finance

Jobs in the financial sector are a significant part of the DC economy. These jobs are closely related to many other booming industries in the district, such as real estate development, economic research, and venture capital, or investing in start-up companies.

5. Library of Congress

The Library of Congress is the national library of the United States and is the largest library in the world. Today the library contains more than 838 miles (1,349 km) of shelves filled with books, photographs, films, and other materials.

6. Museums

The district is home to dozens of museums, which highlight such things as the arts, history, dinosaurs, and spacecraft. The Smithsonian Institution has multiple museums and research centers, which offer a great deal for visitors and residents of all ages.

7. Parks

Washington, DC, is home to many beautiful parks and green spaces. The district contains twenty-three national parks that attract more than thirty-four million visitors each year. The largest DC park, called Rock Creek Park, covers an area of 2,820 acres (1,141 ha).

8. Research

Washington, DC, is an ideal home for research institutions due to the many universities, political groups, and nonprofits in the city. These research groups collect and study information about topics including scientific advances, and social issues.

9. Technology

In 2013, *Forbes* magazine declared Washington, DC, the "new tech hot spot" in the country. These companies create many different kinds of new technology, from computer software to medical devices. In 2014, a "tech corridor" was established in Northwest DC.

10. Tourism

In 2014, research showed that tourists to Washington, DC, spent $6.8 billion in the district. Owners and employees of hotels, restaurants, museums, taxi companies, and stores all benefit from the millions of people who visit the city each year.

Museums

Tourism

Recipe for Veggie Dumplings

Get a taste of DC's thriving Chinese-American community by making your own veggie dumplings at home.

What You Need

One package of wonton wrappers

1 cup (about 100 grams) finely chopped shallots or onion

½ package (about 7 ounces or 200 g) extra firm tofu, drained

1 cup (about 100 g) mushrooms

1 egg

1 teaspoon (5 g) salt

2 tablespoon (30 milliliters) soy sauce

4 cups (about 960 mL) water

What To Do

- Put your water on the stove to boil. Ask a grown-up for help!
- Chop the tofu, mushrooms, and onion into very fine pieces (you can also use a food processor) and place in a mixing bowl.
- Add the egg, salt, and soy sauce to the bowl and mix together well.
- Place a small amount of the mixture—about a tablespoon—onto each wonton wrapper.
- Close each dumpling by folding it over the filling and pinching the edges together to seal.
- Drop the dumplings into the boiling water. Boil for five to eight minutes.
- Use a slotted spoon to scoop the dumplings out and put on a plate to drain.

It connects Washington, DC, with the suburbs where many of the city's workers live, including counties in Maryland and Virginia. The highest ridership ever recorded on the Metro was on the day of President Barack Obama's first inauguration, January 20, 2009. More than 1.1 million riders used the Metro that day.

Interstate highways, including the famous Beltway, carry a huge number of cars and trucks. The Beltway, Interstate 495, encircles Washington, DC, through Maryland and Virginia. The two roadways that make up the Beltway are known as the Inner Loop and Outer Loop. The greater Washington area's three international airports, Ronald Reagan Washington National, Dulles International, and Baltimore/Washington International Thurgood Marshall, together handle more than 2,200 flights a day and 50 million passengers a year.

Manufacturing, Construction, and Technology

Washington, DC, has a small manufacturing industry. Most of the district's manufacturing workers are employed in the printing and publishing industry. They produce newspapers and other publications, as well as printed materials for various parts of the government. Construction is another important segment of the Washington, DC, workforce.

The *Washington Post* is one of the country's most influential newspapers.

Sometimes it seems as if parts of the city are always being improved or rebuilt. In a typical year, thousands of construction workers may be involved in projects around the city.

Many high-tech companies have their headquarters in the Washington area, partly because they need to be close to government agencies that buy their products. Many of these companies, which include software developers and Internet service providers, have chosen to locate in the suburbs. However, in the past few years, there have been signs of high-tech companies moving into the city itself, and many new start-up companies are launching there. Washington's highly-educated workforce, many universities and research institutions, and affordable office space make the city an attractive option for new tech companies. The city and several private groups are working to encourage the growth of this industry by offering grants, tax benefits, and workforce development programs. The district is home to a large number of venture capitalists, investors who provide funding for a company's early years to help them get off the ground in exchange for part of the profits. Non-profit groups like Digital DC help connect new tech companies, or those who want to start a company, with resources that can help them. These resources include government programs, investor groups, and **STEM** education programs that encourage students to go into the fields of science, technology, engineering, or math.

Industries like technology tend to attract young people, and Washington, DC, is no exception. Starting in 2010, new college graduates and others who are part of the millennial generation moved to the district in record numbers. Between 2000 and 2010, the number of people in Washington, DC, between the ages of twenty and thirty-four grew by 23 percent, and in 2010-11 another 10,430 people in that age bracket moved in. With these young people came many benefits to the city's economy. Thousands of new apartment buildings were built, and hundreds of new restaurants and shops were opened. Industries that are popular with young people, like technology and the arts, grew quickly. Government jobs decreased, but jobs in business grew rapidly. Though the number of young people coming to the city has slowed in recent years, this group has made long-lasting contributions and changes to Washington's economy, neighborhoods, and culture.

The Business Of Food

Visitors and residents of Washington, DC, love to eat at restaurants. In 2014, there were 2,144 eating and drinking establishments in the district. Those restaurants account for 60,000 jobs for Washingtonians—or about 8 percent of all employed people in DC.

Looking to the Future

Washington's economy has generally been strong, with the federal government as a steady source of employment. However, in the last few years, Washington, DC, has had one of the nation's highest unemployment rates, with about 7 percent of the district's residents unemployed as of September 2015. The nation's capital has a large number of wealthy people, but it also has a very large number of poor people. In 2008, a number of problems in the world economy caused the beginning of a nationwide **recession**, or period of economic decline. Many people lost their jobs, and companies closed or stopped hiring new people. Because of many factors, including a new president, a new mayor, and the continued need for government services, Washington, DC, was not hit as hard as some other parts of the country. However, the impact of the recession was still felt there. Thankfully, the nation's economy has made great improvements in recent years, and things are starting to look up in Washington and across the United States. Government programs and initiatives to improve the district's economy have helped to improve economic inequalities, though there is still work to do. Washington's challenge, in the years to come, will be to make sure that all its residents share in the wealth and power that make it one of the world's greatest places.

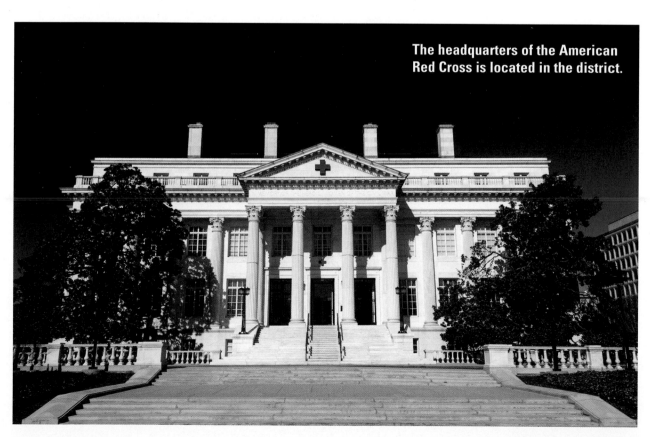

The headquarters of the American Red Cross is located in the district.

WASHINGTON, DC
DISTRICT MAP

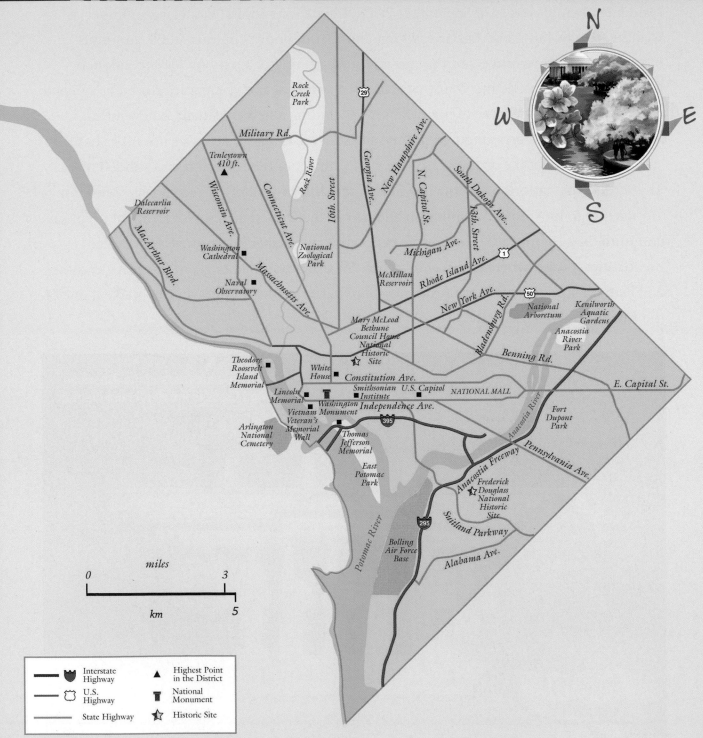

N
W — E
S

Rock Creek Park

US 29

Military Rd.

Tenleytown 410 ft.

Rock River

Wisconsin Ave.

Connecticut Ave.

16th Street

Georgia Ave.

New Hampshire Ave.

N. Capitol St.

South Dakota Ave.

13th Street

Dalecarlia Reservoir

MacArthur Blvd.

Washington Cathedral

Massachusetts Ave.

National Zoological Park

Michigan Ave.

McMillan Reservoir

Rhode Island Ave.

New York Ave.

US 1

US 50

National Arboretum

Kenilworth Aquatic Gardens

Naval Observatory

Bladensburg Rd.

Anacostia River Park

Mary McLeod Bethune Council House National Historic Site

Benning Rd.

Theodore Roosevelt Island Memorial

White House

Constitution Ave.

Smithsonian Institute

U.S. Capitol

NATIONAL MALL

E. Capital St.

Lincoln Memorial

Washington Monument

Independence Ave.

Anacostia River

Vietnam Veteran's Memorial Wall

I-395

Fort Dupont Park

Pennsylvania Ave.

Arlington National Cemetery

Thomas Jefferson Memorial

East Potomac Park

Anacostia Freeway

Frederick Douglass National Historic Site

Suitland Parkway

Potomac River

Bolling Air Force Base

I-295

Alabama Ave.

miles
0   3

km
0   5

	Interstate Highway		▲	Highest Point in the District
	U.S. Highway		▮	National Monument
	State Highway		☆	Historic Site

WASHINGTON, DC
MAP SKILLS

1. The Frederick Douglass National Historic Site is located south of which highway?

2. Arlington National Cemetery is located on which side of the Potomac River?

3. The Washington Cathedral is at the intersection of which two streets?

4. If you wanted to travel from Rock Creek Park to the National Zoological Park, in which direction would you travel?

5. If you traveled west on Military Road from Rock River, what street would you run into first?

6. Bolling Air Force Base is located just west of which major highway?

7. Name the three landmarks on the National Mall that are included in the map.

8. If you traveled south from the Washington Cathedral, which landmark would you reach first?

9. Which body of water is located on the northwest border of Washington, DC?

10. What is the name of the park located south of E. Capital Street?

US Capitol

Naval Observatory

10. Fort Dupont Park
9. Dalecarlia Reservoir
8. Naval Observatory
7. Lincoln Memorial, Smithsonian Institution, US Capitol
6. 295
5. Connecticut Avenue
4. South
3. Wisconsin Avenue and Massachusetts Avenue
2. West
1. Anacostia Freeway

Official Flag, Seal, and Song

The official flag of Washington, DC, is based on George Washington's family coat of arms. It has three red stars and broad red stripes against a white background. The design was chosen by a congressional commission in 1938.

The Washington, DC, seal shows a blindfolded woman—representing justice—laying a wreath at the base of a statue of George Washington. A bald eagle is at her feet, and the sun is rising in the background. At the bottom are the words "Justitia Omnibus," which means "justice for all." Also at the bottom of the seal are the numbers 1871, the year the seal was adopted.

There is disagreement over what the official song of Washington, DC, really is. Some sources list the song as our national anthem, "The Star-Spangled Banner." However, in 1951 a contest was held and composers were asked to write a song for the district. "Washington" by Jimmie Dodd was selected. The song is rarely heard today.

To read the lyrics, visit: **www.dcwatch.com/gary/gri9910.htm#Washington**

Glossary

aqueduct   A human-made channel for carrying water, usually in the form of a bridge supported by tall columns.

archaeologists   Scientist who study human history through the discovery of artifacts and ancient objects.

company town   A place where almost all the stores, houses, and other buildings belong to one company, and where most of the people in town work for that company.

dialect   A form of a language used by people in one location.

federal government   The national government of an entire country, as opposed to the local governments that manage individual states, counties, or cities.

gentrification   Renewal and rebuilding of a neighborhood or area, usually accompanied by a large number of middle-class or affluent people moving to that area.

municipal   Relating to a city or town and the governing body of that location.

nocturnal   Usually used to describe an animal who is mainly active at night.

per capita   Meaning "for each person," it is used as a way of measuring how much of something is divided among the individuals in a population.

quadrant   One part of something that is divided into four equal parts.

recession   A period of temporary economic decline during which trade and industrial activity are reduced.

reverse migration   People moving out of a city or other area that once had a large population.

STEM   An acronym for the academic study of science, technology, engineering, and mathematics.

More About Washington, DC

BOOKS

Clark, Diane C., and Miriam Chernick. *A Kid's Guide to Washington, DC*. Boston: Houghton Mifflin Harcourt, 2008.

Grodin, Elissa. *D is for Democracy: A Citizen's Alphabet*. Ann Arbor, MI: Sleeping Bear Press, 2006.

Korrell, Emily. *Awesome Adventures at the Smithsonian: The Official Kids Guide to the Smithsonian Institution*. Washington, DC: Smithsonian Books, 2013.

Miller, Brandon Marie. *George Washington for Kids: His Life and Times with 21 Activities*. Chicago: Chicago Review Press, 2007.

WEBSITES

America's Story from America's Library

www.americaslibrary.gov

DC Cool Kids

washington.org/dc-cool-kids

The US Government's Official Web Portal for Kids

kids.usa.gov

ABOUT THE AUTHORS

Kerry Jones Waring is a writer and editor from Buffalo, New York, where she lives with her husband and son.

Terry Allan Hicks has contributed to several books in the It's My State! series, and has written other books on US history. He lives in Connecticut with his wife and three children.

Index

Index